MW01706789

Design: Jill Coote
Recipe Photography: Peter Barry
Recipe styling: Jacqueline Bellefontaine,
Helen Burdett, Bridgeen Deery and
Wendy Devenish
Jacket and Illustration Artwork: Jane Winton,
courtesy of Bernard Thornton Artists, London
Compiled and introduced by Laura Potts
Edited by Josephine Bacon

CLB 3352
This edition published in 1994 by
Whitecap Books Ltd., 1086 West 3rd Street,
North Vancouver, B.C., Canada V7P 3JS
© 1993 CLB Publishing,
Godalming, Surrey, England
All rights reserved
Printed and bound in Singapore
ISBN 1-55110-130-0

THE LITTLE BOOK ·OF·

Chicken

RECIPES

A "kitchen gem," giving a wealth of ideas on preparing this versatile and ever-popular meat.

WHITECAP BOOKS

Introduction

Though chicken is now one of our most popular and versatile meats, it is not so long ago that it was considered a luxury, and was reserved by many families as a special treat or as an alternative Sunday roast. Intensive methods of poultry farming, however, have changed this, making chicken both cheaper and more widely available. As a result, chicken is now one of the most frequently eaten meats, making a regular appearance on many people's everyday menus.

The popularity of chicken is due in part to its versatility. The multitude of pre-prepared cuts now available includes legs, thighs, breasts, quarters, and halves, and each of these can be utilized in a wide variety of ways. Some of the best-loved dishes, for example, are hearty stews, which make excellent use of legs and thighs by slowly simmering them with herbs or wine to give a full flavor.

Dishes that use tender breast meat, on the other hand, do not have to be time-consuming and are most successful when the delicate flavor of the meat is enhanced with fresh herbs, a little onion or lemon, or a simple sauce.

The fact that chicken is low in fat and high in protein also plays a large part in its popularity. As people become aware of the health risks presented by a diet high in cholesterol, many make a conscious decision to eat less red meat and switch instead to healthier low-fat protein sources such as chicken.

The recipes in this book have been chosen for their mouthwatering variety, providing inspiration for everyday meals and great ideas for special occasions. They are easy to follow and are accompanied by informative step-by-step pictures, which clarify some of the culinary techniques used.

Chicken Satay

SERVES 4

This typical Indonesian dish is very spicy.

PREPARATION: 25 mins
COOKING: 15 mins

2 tbsps soy sauce
2 tbsps sesame oil
2 tbsps lime juice
1 tsp ground cumin
1 tsp turmeric powder
2 tsps ground coriander
1 pound chicken breast, cut into 1-inch cubes
2 tbsps peanut oil
1 small onion, minced
1 tsp chili powder
½ cup crunchy peanut butter
1 tsp brown sugar
Lime wedges and coriander leaves, for garnish

1. Put the soy sauce, sesame oil, lime juice, cumin, turmeric, and coriander into a large bowl and mix well.

Step 5 Thread the marinated meat onto 4 large, or 8 small, kebob skewers.

2. Add the cubed chicken to the soy sauce marinade, and stir well to coat the meat evenly.

3. Cover and allow to stand in a refrigerator for at least 1 hour, but preferably overnight.

4. Drain the meat, reserving the marinade.

5. Thread the meat onto 4 large or 8 small skewers and set aside.

6. Heat the peanut oil in a small saucepan and add the onion and chili powder. Cook gently until the onion is slightly softened.

7. Stir the reserved marinade into the oil and onion mixture, along with the peanut butter and brown sugar. Heat gently, stirring constantly, until all the ingredients are well blended.

8. If the sauce is too thick, stir in 2-4 tbsps boiling water.

9. Arrange the skewers of meat on a broiler pan and cook under a preheated moderate broiler 10-15 minutes. After the first 5 minutes of cooking, baste the meat with a little peanut sauce.

10. During the cooking time turn the meat frequently to cook it on all sides and prevent it browning.

11. Garnish with the lime and coriander leaves, and serve the remaining sauce separately.

Terrine of Spinach and Chicken

SERVES 6-8

This superb terrine makes a delicious appetizer.

PREPARATION: 25 mins
COOKING: 1 hr

8 ounces chicken breasts, boned and skinned
2 egg whites
1 cup fresh white breadcrumbs
1 pound fresh spinach, washed
1 tbsp each of fresh, finely-chopped chervil, chives and tarragon
Freshly ground black pepper
1¼ cups heavy cream
½ cup finely chopped walnuts
Pinch nutmeg

1. Cut the chicken into small pieces.

2. Put the cut chicken, 1 egg white, and half of the breadcrumbs into a food processor. Blend until well mixed.

3. Put the spinach into a large saucepan, cover with a tight-fitting lid, and cook the spinach 3 minutes, or until it has just wilted.

4. Remove the chicken mixture from the food processor and rinse the bowl.

5. Put the spinach into the food processor along with the herbs, the remaining egg white, and breadcrumbs. Blend until smooth.

6. Season the chicken mixture, and add half of the cream. Mix well to blend thoroughly.

Step 3 The spinach should be cooked until it is just wilted.

7. Add the walnuts, nutmeg, and remaining cream to the spinach and beat well.

8. Line a 1 quart loaf pan with parchment paper. Lightly oil with a little vegetable oil.

9. Pour the chicken mixture into the loaf pan and spread evenly. Carefully pour the spinach mixture over the chicken mixture, and smooth the top.

10. Cover the pan with lightly-oiled aluminum foil and seal tightly around the edges.

11. Stand the pan in a roasting pan and pour enough warm water into the roasting pan to come halfway up the sides. Cook at 325°F for 1 hour, or until firm.

12. Put the terrine into the refrigerator and chill for at least 12 hours.

13. Carefully lift the terrine out of the pan and peel away the paper.

Crumb Fried Chicken

SERVES 6

A tasty dish from Southern Germany.

PREPARATION: 30 mins
COOKING: 40 mins

3-pound chicken
2 eggs, mixed with a pinch of salt
1 cup breadcrumbs
½ cup grated Parmesan cheese
¼ tsp ground ginger
4 tbsps butter or margarine
3 tbsps oil
Lemon and parsley for garnish

1. Preheat the oven to 400°F. To joint the chicken, first cut off the legs, bending them backward to break the joint. Cut in between the joint to completely remove the legs.

2. Cut down the breastbone with sharp poultry shears to separate the two halves. Use the poultry shears to cut through the rib cage. Use the notch in the shears to separate the wing joints from the back.

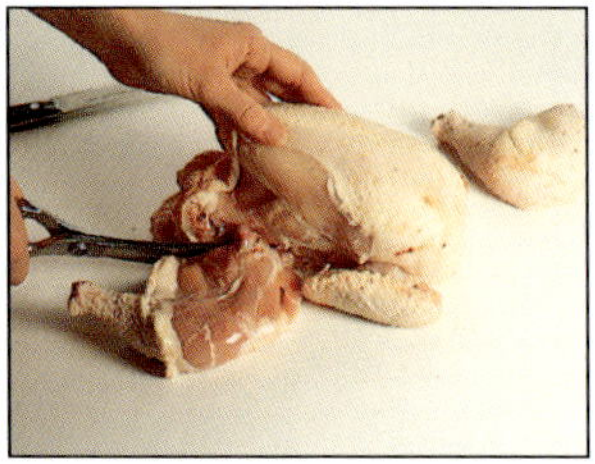

Step 1 Bend the leg backwards to break the ball and socket joint and cut in between.

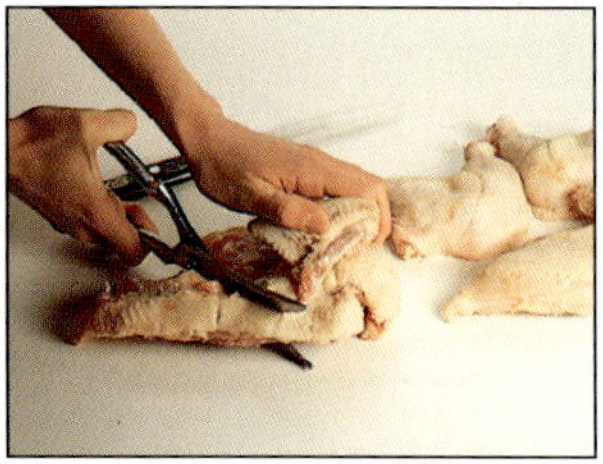

Step 2 Use the notch to cut through the wing joint.

3. Cut the quarters into two pieces each. Use a sharp knife to separate the drumstick from the thigh. Cut the breasts in half, leaving some of the white meat attached to the wing joint. Cut through the bones with poultry shears.

4. Mix the breadcrumbs, Parmesan cheese, and ground ginger together. First dip the chicken into the egg and then coat with the crumbs.

5. Heat the oil in a large skillet and add the butter. When hot, add the chicken, skin side down first. Cook both sides until golden brown.

6. Transfer with a slotted spoon to a baking tray and bake in the oven 20-30 minutes, or until the juices run clear when tested with a knife. Serve garnished with small bunches of parsley, and lemon wedges or slices.

Saffron Chicken

SERVES 4

Saffron gives rice and sauces a lovely golden color and delicate taste.

PREPARATION: 20-25 mins
COOKING: 25-35 mins

2 tbsps oil
2-3 pound chicken, cut into 8 pieces and skinned if desired
1 small onion, finely chopped
2 tsps paprika
1 clove garlic, crushed
8 tomatoes, peeled, seeded and chopped
1¼ cups rice
3 cups boiling water
Large pinch saffron or ¼ tsp ground saffron
¾ cup frozen green peas
2 tbsps chopped parsley

1. Heat the oil in a large skillet. Season the chicken and place it in the hot oil, skin side down first. Cook over moderate heat, turning the chicken frequently to brown it lightly. Set the chicken aside.

2. Add the onions to the oil and cook slowly until softened but not colored.

3. Add the paprika and cook about 2 minutes, stirring frequently until the paprika loses some of its red color. Add the garlic and the tomatoes.

Step 4 When the garlic and tomatoes are added, cook over a high heat to evaporate the liquid.

4. Cook the mixture over high heat about 5 minutes to evaporate the liquid from the tomatoes. The mixture should be of dropping consistency when done. Transfer the mixture to a casserole or Dutch oven, add the rice, water, and saffron and stir together.

5. Add the chicken to the casserole and bring to the boil over high heat. Reduce to simmering, cover tightly, and cook about 20 minutes. Remove chicken, and add the peas and parsley. Cook a further 5-10 minutes, or until rice is tender. Combine with the chicken to serve.

Chicken Cacciatore

SERVES 4-6

A rich Italian dish with mushrooms and olives.

PREPARATION: 30 mins
COOKING: 1hr 15 mins

3 tbsps oil
1 cup mushrooms, quartered if large
3 pounds chicken pieces
1 onion
2 cloves garlic
⅔ cup vermouth
1 tbsp white wine vinegar
⅔ cup chicken broth
1 tsp oregano
1 sprig fresh rosemary
1 pound canned tomatoes
¼ cup black olives, pitted
2 tbsps chopped parsley

1. Heat the oil in a heavy-based skillet and cook the mushrooms about 1-2 minutes. Remove them and set aside.

2. Brown the chicken in the oil and transfer the browned pieces to an ovenproof casserole.

3. Mince the onion and garlic. Pour away all but 1 tbsp of the oil in the skillet and reheat the pan. Cook the onion and garlic until softened but not colored.

4. Add the vermouth and vinegar and boil to reduce by half.

5. Add the chicken broth, tomatoes, oregano, rosemary, and season. Break up the tomatoes and bring the sauce to the boil. Allow to cook 2 minutes.

6. Pour the sauce over the chicken in the casserole, cover, and cook in a preheated 350°F oven about 1 hour.

7. To pit the olives, roll them on a flat surface to loosen the stones and then use a swivel vegetable peeler to extract them. Alternatively use a cherry-pitter.

8. Add mushrooms and olives during the last 5 minutes of cooking.

9. Remove the rosemary before serving and sprinkle with chopped parsley.

Step 3 Cut onion in half lengthwise leaving root end intact. Cut in thin crosswise slices. Then cut in lengthwise strips.

Chicken Cobbler

SERVES 6

A warming winter dish with a creamy sauce and biscuit topping.

PREPARATION: 25 mins
COOKING: 1 hr

4 chicken pieces, 2 breasts and 2 legs
1½ pints water
1 bayleaf
4 whole peppercorns
2 carrots, peeled and diced
24 pearl onions, peeled
6 tbsps frozen corn kernels
⅔ cup heavy cream

Topping
3½ cups all-purpose flour
1½ tbsps baking powder
Pinch salt
5 tbsps butter or margarine
1½ cups milk
1 egg, beaten with a pinch of salt

1. Place the chicken in a deep saucepan or Dutch oven with water, bayleaf, and peppercorns. Cover and bring to the boil. Reduce the heat and allow to simmer 20-30 minutes, or until the chicken is tender. Remove the chicken from the pot and allow to cool. Skim and discard the fat from the surface of the broth. Skin the chicken and remove the meat from the bones.

Step 5 Roll out the mixture on a floured surface, cut into rounds and place on top of the chicken mixture.

2. Continue to simmer the broth until reduced by about half. Strain, then add the carrots and onions. Cook until tender and add the corn. Stir in the cream and season. Add the chicken. Pour into a casserole.

3. To prepare the topping, sift the dry ingredients into a bowl.

4. Rub in the butter or margarine until the mixture resembles small peas. Stir in enough of the milk to bind the mixture.

5. Turn out onto a floured surface and knead lightly. Roll out with a floured rolling pin and cut into rounds with a cookie cutter. Brush the surface of each round with the egg mixture. Place on top of the chicken mixture and bake 10-15 minutes in a pre-heated oven at 375°F. Serve immediately.

Country Captain Chicken

SERVES 6

This dish was named for a sea captain with a taste for the spicy cuisine of India.

PREPARATION: 30 mins
COOKING: 50 mins

3 pounds chicken pieces
Seasoned flour
6 tbsps oil
1 medium onion, chopped
1 medium green bell pepper, seeded and chopped
1 clove garlic, crushed
2 tsps curry powder
3½ cups canned tomatoes
2 tsps chopped parsley
1 tsp chopped marjoram
4 tbsps raisins
¼ cup blanched almond halves

1. Remove skin from the chicken and dredge with flour, shaking off the excess.

Step 4 Add the curry powder to the vegetables in the skillet and cook two minutes over low heat, stirring frequently.

Step 5 Toast the almonds on a baking tray in the oven until light golden brown.

2. Heat the oil and brown the chicken on all sides until golden. Remove to an ovenproof casserole.

3. Pour off all but 2 tbsps of the oil. Add the onion, pepper, and garlic and cook slowly to soften.

4. Add the curry powder and season. Cook, stirring frequently, for 2 minutes. Add the tomatoes, parsley, and marjoram and bring to the boil. Pour the sauce over the chicken, cover and cook in a pre-heated 350°F oven for 45 minutes. Add the currants or raisins during the last 15 minutes.

5. Meanwhile, toast the almonds in the oven on a baking tray along with the chicken. Stir them frequently and watch carefully. Sprinkle over the chicken just before serving.

Chicken with Olives

SERVES 4-6

This is a chicken sauté dish for olive lovers. Use more or less of them as your own taste dictates.

PREPARATION: 25 mins
COOKING: 50-55 mins

3 pounds chicken pieces
2 tbsps olive oil
2 tbsps butter or margarine
1 clove garlic, crushed
⅔ cup white wine
⅔ cup chicken stock
2 tbsps chopped parsley
20 pitted black and green olives
4 zucchini, cut in ½-inch pieces

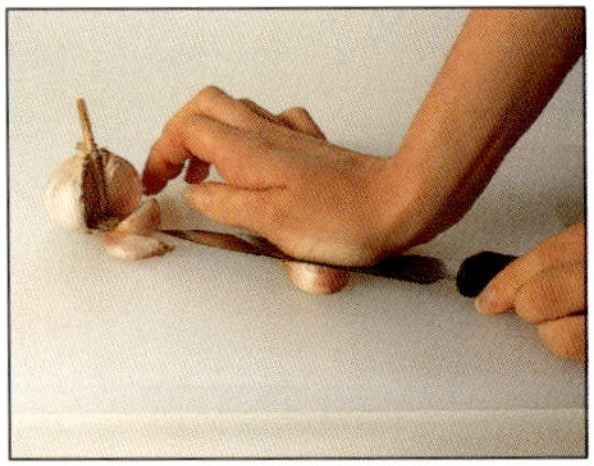

To peel a garlic clove easily, first crush it gently with the blunt side of a large knife. The skin will split, making it easier to remove.

Step 1 Cook the chicken, skin side down first, until golden brown.

1. Heat the oil in a large skillet and add the butter or margarine. When foaming, add the chicken, skin side down. Brown one side of the chicken and turn over to brown the other side. Cook the chicken in two batches if necessary.

2. Turn the chicken skin side up, and add the garlic, wine, and stock, season, then bring to the boil. Cover the pan and allow to simmer over gentle heat about 30-35 minutes.

3. Add the zucchini and cook 10 minutes. Once the chicken and zucchini are done, add the olives and cook to heat through. Add the parsley and remove to a dish to serve.

Chicken with Eggplant and Ham Stuffing

SERVES 4-6

Eggplant and ham make an unusual stuffing and add interest to roast chicken.

PREPARATION: 30 mins
COOKING: 5-6 mins for the stuffing and about 1 hr for the chicken

3-pound frying chicken
1 small eggplant
4 tbsps butter
1 small onion, finely chopped
½ cup chopped, lean ham
1 cup fresh breadcrumbs
2 tsps dried chopped mixed herbs
1-2 eggs, beaten

1. Cut the eggplant in half lengthwise and remove stem. Lightly score the surface with a sharp knife and sprinkle with salt. Leave to stand for about 30 minutes for the salt to draw out any bitter juices.

2. Melt half the butter in a saucepan and cook the onion slowly to soften slightly.

Step 1 Sprinkle the cut surface of the eggplant lightly with salt and leave to stand.

Step 4 Remove the fat from just inside the cavity opening.

3. Rinse the eggplant and pat dry. Cut into ½-inch cubes. Cook with the onion until fairly soft. Add the remaining stuffing ingredients, beating in the egg gradually until the mixture just holds together. Season to taste.

4. Remove the fat from just inside the chicken cavity. Fill the neck end with some of the stuffing. Place any extra in a greased casserole. Tuck the wing tips under the chicken to hold the neck flap down. Tie the legs together and place the chicken in a roasting pan.

5. Spread with the remaining softened butter and roast in a pre-heated 350°F oven for about 1 hour, or until the juices from the chicken run clear when the thickest part of the thigh is pierced with a sharp knife. Cook extra stuffing, covered for the last 35 minutes of cooking time. Leave the chicken to stand for 10 minutes before carving. If desired, make a gravy with the pan juices.

Spicy Spanish Chicken

SERVES 6

Chili peppers, coriander (cilantro) and tomatoes add a Spanish flavor to broiled chicken.

PREPARATION: 1 hr
COOKING: 14-20 mins

6 boned chicken breasts
Grated rind and juice of 1 lime
2 tbsps olive oil
6 tbsps whole grain mustard
2 tsps paprika
4 ripe tomatoes, peeled, seeded, and quartered
2 shallots, chopped
1 clove garlic, crushed
½ chili pepper, seeded and chopped
1 tsp wine vinegar
2 tbsps chopped fresh coriander (cilantro)
Whole coriander (cilantro) leaves to garnish

1. Place chicken breasts in a shallow dish with the lime rind and juice, oil, mustard, paprika, and coarsely ground black pepper. Marinate

Step 2 Tomatoes peel easily when placed first in boiling water and then in cold.

Step 4 Broil skin side of chicken until brown and crisp before turning pieces over.

about 1 hour, turning occasionally.

2. To peel tomatoes easily, drop them into boiling water for about 5 seconds or less depending on ripeness. Place immediately in cold water. Skins should peel away easily.

3. Coarsely chop tomatoes, shallots, garlic, chili pepper, then add the vinegar and salt. Stir in the coriander (cilantro).

4. Place chicken on a broiler pan and reserve the marinade. Cook chicken, skin side uppermost, about 7-10 minutes, depending on how close the chicken is to the heat source. Baste frequently with the remaining marinade. Broil other side in the same way. Sprinkle with salt after broiling.

5. Place chicken on serving plates and garnish with coriander (cilantro) leaves. Serve with a spoonful of the tomato relish on the side.

Lime Roasted Chicken

SERVES 4

Its simple, tangy flavor make this an ideal summer dish.

PREPARATION: 25 mins, plus 4 hrs to marinate
COOKING: 40 mins

4 chicken breast portions
4 limes
2 tsps white wine vinegar
5 tbsps olive oil
2 tsp fresh chopped basil

1. Rub the chicken portions all over with salt and black pepper. Place in a shallow ovenproof dish, and set aside.

2. Carefully pare away thin strips of the rind from only 2 of the limes, using a lemon parer. Cut these 2 limes in half and squeeze the juice.

3. Add the lime juice to the vinegar and 4 tbsps of the olive oil in a small dish, along with the strips of rind, and mix well.

4. Pour the oil and lime juice mixture over the chicken. Cover and refrigerate at least 4 hours or overnight.

Step 5 After marinating for 4 hours, the chicken will look slightly cooked and the meat will have turned a pale opaque color.

Step 7 Sauté the lime slices very quickly in the hot oil until they just begin to soften.

5. Remove the covering from the dish in which the chicken is marinating, and baste the chicken well with the marinade mixture. Place in a preheated 375°F oven and cook 30-35 minutes, or until the chicken is well-roasted and tender.

6. In the meantime, peel away the rind and white parts from the remaining 2 limes. Cut the limes into thin slices using a sharp knife.

7. Heat the remaining oil in a small skillet and add the lime slices and basil. Cook quickly 1 minute, or until the fragrance rises up from the basil and the limes just begin to soften.

8. Serve the chicken portions on a serving platter, garnished with the fried lime slices and a little fresh basil.

Chicken and Pepper Salad

SERVES 6

This piquant lunch or light supper dish can be prepared in advance.

PREPARATION: 30 mins

1 pound cooked chicken, cut in strips
⅔ cup mayonnaise
⅔ cup plain yogurt
1 tsp chili powder
1 tsp paprika
Pinch cayenne pepper
½ tsp tomato paste
1 tsp onion paste
1 green bell pepper, seeded and finely sliced
1 red bell pepper, seeded and finely sliced
1 cup frozen sweetcorn, defrosted
1 cup cooked long grain rice

Step 2 Fold all ingredients together gently so that they do not break up. Use a large spoon or rubber spatula.

Step 4 Arrange rice on a serving platter and spoon salad into the center.

1. Place the chicken strips in a large salad bowl.

2. Mix the mayonnaise, yogurt, spices, tomato paste, and onion purée together and leave to stand briefly for flavors to blend. Fold dressing into the chicken.

3. Add the peppers and sweetcorn and mix gently until all the ingredients are coated with dressing.

4. Place the rice on a serving platter and pile the salad into the center. Serve immediately.

Chicken and Avocado Salad

SERVES 4

The creamy herb dressing complements this easy summer salad.

PREPARATION: 30 mins

8 anchovy fillets, soaked in milk, rinsed and dried
1 green onion (scallion), chopped
2 tbsps chopped fresh tarragon
3 tbsps chopped chives
4 tbsps chopped parsley
1¼ cups mayonnaise
⅔ cup plain yogurt
2 tbsps tarragon vinegar
Pinch sugar and cayenne pepper
1 large Boston or iceberg lettuce
1 pound cooked chicken
1 avocado, peeled and cubed
1 tbsp lemon juice

Step 1 The dressing should be very well blended after working in a food processor. Alternatively, use a hand blender.

Step 3 Arrange lettuce on individual plates and top with shredded chicken.

1. Combine all the ingredients, except the lettuce, avocado, and chicken in a food processor. Work the ingredients until smooth, and well mixed. Leave in the refrigerator at least 1 hour for the flavors to blend.

2. Shred the lettuce or tear into bite-size pieces and arrange on plates.

3. Top the lettuce with the cooked chicken cut into strips or cubes.

4. Spoon the dressing over the chicken. Toss the avocado cubes with lemon juice and garnish the salad. Serve any remaining dressing separately.

Tarragon Chicken Pancakes

SERVES 4

These easy-to-make pancakes are sophisticated enough for a dinner party.

PREPARATION: 25 mins
COOKING: 25 mins

Pancake batter
4 ounces wholewheat flour
1 egg
1¼ cups milk
Oil for frying

Filling
3 tbsps all-purpose flour
1¼ cups skim milk
1 cup skinned, chopped cooked chicken
1 avocado, peeled, halved, pitted and chopped
2 tsps lemon juice
1 tbsp chopped fresh tarragon

1. Sift the wholewheat flour into a large bowl, and make a slight well in the center. Break the egg into the well and begin to beat it carefully into the flour, incorporating only a little flour at a time.

2. Add the milk gradually to the egg and flour mixture, beating well between additions, until all the milk is incorporated and the batter is smooth.

3. Heat a little oil in a small skillet, or omelet pan and cook about 2 tbsps of the batter at a time, tipping and rotating the pan, so that the batter spreads evenly over the base to form a

Step 3 Using a small skillet or omelet pan, heat a little oil and fry 2 tbsps of the batter at a time.

pancake. Flip the pancake over, to cook the other side.

4. Repeat this process until all the batter has been used. Keep the pancakes warm until required.

5. Blend the all-purpose flour with a little of the milk, then gradually add the rest of the milk.

6. Pour the flour-and-milk mixture into a small pan, and cook over a moderate heat, stirring continuously, until the sauce has thickened. Season to taste.

7. Stir the chopped chicken, avocado, lemon juice, and tarragon into the sauce.

8. Fold each pancake in half, and then in half again, to form a triangle.

9. Carefully open part of the triangle out to form an envelope, and fill this with the chicken and avocado mixture.

Eggplant and Chicken Chili

SERVES 4

This unusual stir-fry dish is both delicious and filling.

PREPARATION: 10 mins
COOKING: 15 mins

2 medium-sized eggplants
4 tbsps sesame oil
2 cloves garlic, peeled and crushed
4 green onions (scallions)
1 green chili pepper, finely chopped
12 ounces boned and skinned chicken breast
4 tbsps light soy sauce
2 tbsps broth or water
1 tbsp tomato paste
1 tsp cornstarch
1 tsp sugar

1. Cut the eggplant into quarters lengthwise, using a sharp knife. Slice the eggplant quarters into pieces approximately ½-inch thick.

2. Put the eggplant slices into a bowl and sprinkle liberally with salt. Stir well to coat evenly. Cover with plastic wrap and leave to stand 30 minutes.

3. Rinse the eggplant slices very thoroughly under running water, then pat dry with a clean kitchen towel.

4. Heat half of the oil in a wok or large skillet, and gently cook the garlic until it is soft, but not colored.

5. Add the eggplant slices to the wok and cook, stirring frequently, 3-4 minutes.

Step 6 Cut the green onions (scallions) diagonally into small pieces, approximately ½ inch long.

6. Slice the green onions (scallions) into thin diagonal strips. Stir into the cooked eggplant together with the chili, and cook 1 minute. Remove the eggplant and onion and set aside, keeping warm.

7. Cut the chicken breast into thin slices with a sharp knife.

8. Heat the remaining oil in the wok, and fry the chicken pieces approximately 2 minutes or until they have turned white and are cooked through.

9. Return the eggplant and onions to the pan and cook, stirring continuously, 2 minutes or until heated through completely.

10. Mix together the remaining ingredients and pour these over the chicken and eggplant in the wok, stirring constantly until the sauce has thickened and cleared. Serve immediately.

Chicken Liver Stir-Fry

SERVES 4

Chicken livers need quick cooking, so they are a perfect choice for the Chinese stir-fry

PREPARATION: 25 mins
COOKING: 4-5 mins

8 ounces chicken livers
3 tbsps oil
2 ounces split blanched almonds
1 clove garlic, peeled
2 ounces snow peas
8-10 Chinese (Nappa) cabbage
2 tsps cornstarch
2 tbsps soy sauce
¼ cup chicken broth

1. Pick over the chicken livers and remove any discolored areas or bits of fat. Cut the chicken livers into even-sized pieces.

2. Heat a wok and add the oil. When the oil is hot, reduce the heat and add the almonds.

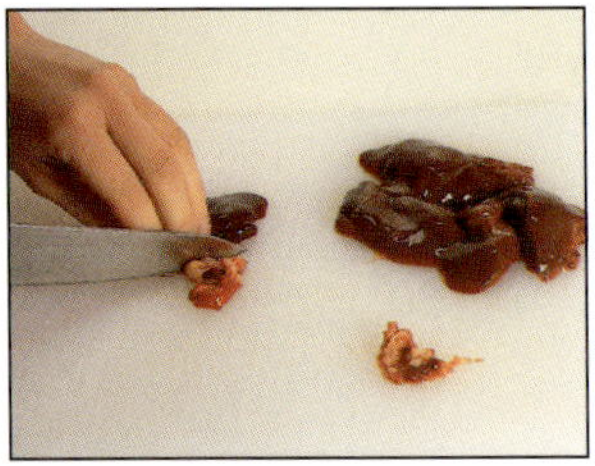

Step 1 Cut off any yellowish or greenish portions from the livers and divide them into even-sized pieces.

Step 3 Quickly stir-fry the livers until lightly browned on the outside. They may be served slightly pink in the center.

Cook, stirring continuously, over gentle heat until the almonds are a nice golden brown. Remove and drain on paper towels.

3. Add the garlic, cook 1-2 minutes to flavor the oil and remove. Add the chicken livers and cook about 2-3 minutes, stirring frequently. Remove the chicken livers and set them aside. Add the snow peas to the wok and stir-fry 1 minute. Shred the Chinese (Nappa) cabbage finely, add to the wok and cook 1 minute. Remove the vegetables and set them aside.

4. Mix the cornstarch with a little water and the soy sauce and broth. Pour into the wok and bring to the boil. Cook until thickened and clear. Return all the other ingredients to the sauce and reheat 30 seconds. Serve immediately.

Cornish Hens with Devilled Sauce

SERVES 4

Although this recipe takes quite a while to prepare, the end result will make your effort worthwhile.

PREPARATION: 25 mins, plus 1 hr standing time
COOKING: 60-70 mins.

4 Cornish hens
1 tsp each of paprika, mustard powder, and ground ginger
½ tsp ground turmeric
¼ tsp ground allspice
4 tbsps unsalted butter
2 tbsps chili sauce
1 tbsp plum sauce (optional)
1 tbsp brown sauce*
1 tbsp Worcestershire sauce
1 tbsp soy sauce
Dash Tabasco sauce
3 tbsps chicken broth

1. Tie the legs of each poussin together and tuck them under the wing tips.

2. Put the paprika, mustard powder, ginger, turmeric and allspice into a small bowl and mix together well.

3. Rub the spice mixture evenly on all sides of the four Cornish hens, taking great care to push some behind the wings and into the joints.

4. Refrigerate the Cornish hens for at least 1 hour.

Step 3 Rub the Cornish hens all over with the spice mixture, pressing it down into the wings and joints.

5. Arrange the Cornish hens in a roasting pan. Melt the butter and brush it evenly over the birds. Roast in a preheated 350°F oven 20 minutes, brushing with the roasting juices during this time.

6. In a small bowl, mix together the chili sauce, plum sauce, brown sauce, Worcestershire sauce, soy sauce, Tabasco and chicken broth.

7. Brush about half of this sauce over the Cornish hens. Return to the oven and cook a further 40 minutes.

8. Brush the Cornish hens twice more with the remaining sauce mixture during this final cooking time so that the skins become brown and crisp.

*Brown sauce is a thick, spicy sauce available in the gourmet section of the supermarket. There are various brands, such as OK, Pickapeppa, etc.

Chicken with Cloud Ears

SERVES 6

Cloud ears is the delightful name for an edible tree fungus which is mushroom-like in taste and texture.

PREPARATION: 25 mins
COOKING: 5 mins

---

12 cloud ears, wood ears or other dried Chineese mushrooms, soaked in boiling water 5 minutes
1 pound boned chicken breasts, thinly sliced
1 egg white
2 tsps cornstarch
2 tsps white wine
2 tsps sesame oil
1 inch piece fresh ginger root, left whole
1 clove garlic, left whole
1¼ cups oil
1¼ cups chicken broth
1 tbsp cornstarch
3 tbsps light soy sauce

Step 1 Soak mushrooms in boiling water five minutes.

1. Soak the mushrooms until they soften and swell. Remove the skin from the chicken and cut into thin slices. Mix the chicken with egg white, cornstarch, wine, and sesame oil.

2. Heat the wok for a few minutes and pour in the oil. Add the whole piece of ginger and whole garlic clove to the oil and cook about 1 minute. Take them out and reduce the heat.

3. Add about a quarter of the chicken at a time and stir-fry about 1 minute. Remove and continue cooking until all the chicken is fried. Drain off excess oil, leaving 2 tbsps in the wok.

4. Drain the mushrooms and squeeze them to extract all the liquid. If using mushrooms with stems, discard the stems before slicing thinly. Cut into smaller pieces. Add to the wok and cook about 1 minute. Add the broth and allow it to come almost to the boil. Mix together the cornstarch and soy sauce and add a spoonful of the hot broth. Add the mixture to the wok, stirring constantly, and bring to the boil. Allow to boil 1-2 minutes or until thickened and clear.

5. Return the chicken to the wok and season. Stir thoroughly about 1 minute and serve immediately.

Index

Lime Roasted Chicken, a tangy, low-calorie dish